T 8669

1442

	DATE DUE		
AUG 21 1989			
DEC 7 - '92			
JUL 03 '93			
JUL 21 '93			
JAN 18 1999			
MAR. 21 2005			

Discovering

DEER

Jill Bailey

The Bookwright Press
New York · 1988

Discovering Nature

Discovering Ants
Discovering Bees and Wasps
Discovering Beetles
Discovering Birds of Prey
Discovering Butterflies and Moths
Discovering Crabs and Lobsters
Discovering Crickets and Grasshoppers
Discovering Damselflies and Dragonflies
Discovering Deer
Discovering Ducks and Geese
Discovering Flies
Discovering Flowering Plants

Discovering Foxes
Discovering Freshwater Fish
Discovering Frogs and Toads
Discovering Fungi
Discovering Rabbits and Hares
Discovering Rats and Mice
Discovering Saltwater Fish
Discovering Sea Birds
Discovering Slugs and Snails
Discovering Snakes and Lizards
Discovering Spiders
Discovering Squirrels
Discovering Worms

Further titles are in preparation

First published in the
United States in 1988 by
The Bookwright Press
387 Park Avenue South
New York, NY 10016

First published in 1988 by
Wayland (Publishers) Limited
61 Western Road, Hove
East Sussex BN3 1JD, England

© Copyright 1988 Wayland (Publishers) Limited

ISBN 0-531–18196–0
Library of Congress Catalog Card Number: 87–73167

Typeset by DP Press Ltd., Sevenoaks, Kent
Printed in Italy by Sagdos S.p.A., Milan

14442

Cover *Two wapiti bulls in Yellowstone National Park.*

Frontispiece *A fallow deer stag in Richmond Park near London, England. Its summer coat is reddish with white spots.*

Contents

1
Introducing Deer

The musk deer stag has a pair of long tusk-like teeth in its upper jaw, like its early ancestors.

Origins and Relatives

Deer are furry animals with long slender legs, quite long necks, narrow heads and short tails. Their feet end in hard hoofs. They range in size from as small as a rabbit to as big as a horse. At certain times of year, male deer grow branching, horn-like structures on their heads called **antlers**.

Deer belong to a large group of warm-blooded animals called **mammals**. Their closest relatives are cattle, giraffes and antelopes. These animals all have hoofs that are divided in two. Their footprints look like pairs of crescent-shaped dents. They are either **grazing** animals, feeding on grasses and other plants that grow close to the ground, or **browsers**, reaching up to feed on leaves and twigs.

Deer have existed for a very long time. The first deer-like animals appeared about 35 million years ago. The early ancestors of the deer did not have antlers, just small, fur-covered bumps on their heads rather like those of the giraffe. Some of them had long teeth that formed tusks instead. A few kinds of deer still have such tusks today. Later, deer with antlers appeared. Some grew very big. Until about 10,000 years ago, there were giant deer with huge antlers that measured over 3½ meters (10 ft) from tip to tip, and weighed more than 40 kilos (90 lb).

A mule deer buck and hind. Deer are the only animals that grow antlers. The mule deer's name comes from its mule-like ears.

The European giant deer, which lived during the ice age, had the largest antlers on record.

What Deer Look Like

Deer are graceful animals with long legs. Male deer, called **bucks** or **stags**, grow large, branching, bony antlers on their heads in the **breeding season**. These are used to threaten and fight other males, and to defend themselves against wolves and other enemies.

Most deer have brownish coats, with lighter underparts. This color blends well with their surroundings and makes deer very difficult to spot. Most deer have a light patch of fur around the rump. The tail may be very short and thick, or it may be thin with a tassel on the end. The coat is **molted** and renewed twice a year. In cold climates, the winter coat is thicker than the summer coat.

Deer have large ears that they can move to pick up sound from different directions. This is important for detecting danger. They have a very good sense of smell, and their noses are hairless and moist. Deer use smell to find food, to recognize friends and

An axis deer buck or chital, also called the spotted deer of India, from the swamps of Asia. The chital is one of the few deer that has a spotted coat. In its natural home the spots help to break up its outline so that it is not easy to detect.

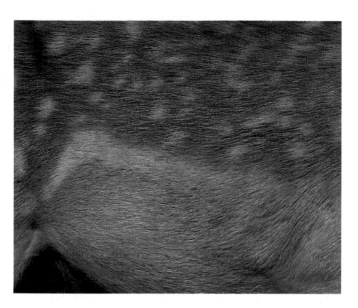

The spotted coat of a fallow deer. Deer usually have a tough, waterproof outer layer of hairs, with a softer, warmer layer underneath.

The smallest deer is the pudu, which is only about 30 cm (11 in) high at the shoulder. The largest is the moose, called the elk in Europe, which is about 2 m (6 ft) tall.

mates, and to detect danger. They do not have good eyesight. They see only a black-and-white world, and the picture is not very sharp. But deer are very good at detecting the smallest movement in their surroundings.

A deer's feet have only four toes. The third and fourth toes form the hoof, a hard, horny small structure that allows the deer to run very fast. The other two toes are short, and do not reach the ground.

Antlers

Deer are the only animals that grow antlers. Only the males of most kinds of deer grow antlers, but both male and female caribou and reindeer grow them. Musk deer and Chinese water deer do not have antlers, but the males have small sharp tusks instead.

Antlers grow from a ridge of bone on the top of the head, between the ears. They are the fastest growing structures known in any animal. Antlers look like large branching horns, but they are actually made of bone. When they first start to grow, they are covered with soft silky fur called **velvet**. Under this fur the skin contains many blood vessels to supply

A deer's antlers are covered with velvety fur while they grow. Fallow deer have wide flat antlers with points that look somewhat like fingers on a hand.

food to the growing antlers. When the antlers are fully grown, the velvet starts to rot and peel off. This attracts flies, and the deer seems to find it itchy. It rubs its antlers on bushes and twigs to get rid of the velvet and to polish the antlers.

This caribou bull is being annoyed by flies while the velvet peels off his full-grown antlers.

After the breeding season, the antlers drop off, one at a time. They grow again before the following breeding season.

Different kinds of deer have antlers with different patterns of branching. Some have wide flat antlers with points along their edges, others have thinner, many-branched antlers. Muntjac deer have short simple antlers on long furry pegs.

The muntjac deer has short simple antlers on long furry pegs.

2
Where Deer Live

A mule deer stretches up to feed on pine needles. Many deer feed on trees as well as grazing on grass.

Woodlands and Grasslands

Deer can be found on every continent except Antarctica and southern Africa. In Britain and North America they are the commonest large wild animals.

Most deer live in woodlands and forests, where they feed on leaves, twigs, flowers and fruits. They may leave the woods to feed in more open country at dawn and dusk, when they are less likely to be seen by their enemies. Deer are very shy animals, and their brown coats provide such good **camouflage** among the tree trunks and the dead leaves on the forest floor that they are seldom seen.

The woodlands of North America are home to the white-tailed deer, the mule deer and the black-tailed deer. Muntjac, chital, sambar, Sika deer and musk deer live in the forests of Asia and the Far East, and the tiny pudu is

A white-tailed buck lies in the sun in its natural woodland home.

been destroyed, red deer have taken to living on the open moorland.

Only a few kinds of deer live in open grasslands where there are few bushes or trees to hide them from their enemies. They usually lie low in the long grass or retreat to nearby woodlands by day, coming out to feed at dusk.

found only in very dense forest in the South American Andes.

Where woodlands have been cleared for farmland, deer often venture into the fields, feeding on the crops. The red deer, found in Britain, Europe and Asia, is really a woodland animal, but in the Highlands of Scotland, where the old forests have

A mule deer rests in the long grass.

Swamps

Wet swampy ground often has a very lush growth of grass and other plants, and some kinds of deer have become **adapted** for living in wet places. The little Chinese water deer, which is only 50 centimeters (20 in) tall at the shoulder, lives in reed beds and swamps. It feeds on grasses and

Moose and European elk often wade into the water to feed.

sedges. The Indian swamp deer has wide spreading hoofs to support it on the soft wet ground. The hog deer lives in the flooded paddy fields of the Far East, feeding on the young rice plants.

The largest living deer, the moose (called the elk in Europe), lives in the northern forests of North America, Europe and Asia. It often feeds near lakes, streams and marshes, sometimes wading chest deep to feed on water plants. The moose will even dive in search of water plants, staying under water for half a minute at a time. It is a powerful swimmer, and can swim for several miles without stopping, paddling with its hoofs. The hairs of the moose's coat are hollow and filled with air, which helps it to stay afloat. The moose's large spreading feet not only support it on boggy ground, but also help to prevent it from sinking in the winter snow.

The rare marsh deer lives in the swamps of South America. Its webbed, wide-spreading hoofs prevent it from sinking in the mud.

During the breeding season the Père David's deer from the royal parks of China wades into the water, and tears up water plants with his antlers, until he is wearing a crown of trailing water weeds.

A Père David's deer rests with his harem.

Mountains and Tundra

In the far north, beyond the northern forests, lies the **tundra**, a wide treeless land covered in low-growing plants and **lichens**. These provide food for large herds of North American caribou and their close relatives, the reindeer of Europe and the U.S.S.R. One particular kind of lichen is so popular among the reindeer and caribou that it has been nicknamed "reindeer moss."

In the autumn, caribou travel hundreds of miles south to the shelter of the forests.

Before the bitter Arctic winter arrives, the reindeer and caribou **migrate** hundreds of miles south to the shelter of the forests.

High mountain tops have a climate and plants similar to those of the tundra. Mule deer live in the Rocky Mountains, and guemal are found as high as 4,000 meters (13,000 ft) in the Andes of South America. The tufted deer of Asia lives even higher. The tiny pudu, the world's smallest deer, lives in the Andes, but prefers the dense cover of the high mountain forests.

Mountain tops and tundra become bitterly cold in winter, so the deer shed their summer coats and grow thicker coats in winter. The outer hairs form a waterproofing layer, and the fur below is soft and warm. These winter coats are paler than the summer coats, giving better camouflage in the frost and snow.

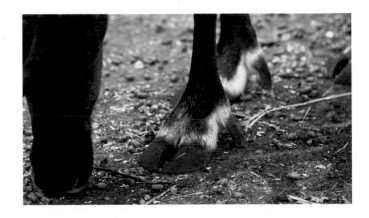

The reindeer has large, spreading feet, which help to prevent it from sinking in marshy ground or in snow.

A mule deer feeds on grass on a mountain in Olympic National Park.

3
Deer on the Move

Caribou often cross rivers on their long journeys to and from the tundra.

Caribou and reindeer live in the far north. They are the only deer that live in vast herds numbering hundreds, sometimes thousands, of animals. In the summer they feed on the tundra, the treeless country beyond the great forests.

In the winter, the tundra is frozen, and the low-growing plants – the deer's food – are buried under deep snow. In the autumn, caribou and reindeer travel south to the shelter of the forests. During this journey, they **court** and mate. They travel up to 1,000 kilometers (600 mi), always using the same routes. These journeys are called migrations.

In the forests, the snow is not frozen, and the caribou can dig for food. By the spring, the females are large and heavy with the young developing inside them. Before the snow has melted, they start the long trek north, back to the tundra. A migrating herd of caribou may spread out over 300 kilometers (200 mi).

On the way, they stop at a special place to give birth to their young. A few weeks later, the young are able to fend for themselves, and the herds move on again.

Winter in the mountains is also bitterly cold, and strong icy winds sweep the slopes. Mountain deer, like the European elk, the wapiti and the mule deer, move down to the shelter of the grassy valleys in winter. In spring they will return to feed on the new grass of the alpine meadows.

A wapiti, or American elk, in Yellowstone National Park. It has moved down from the high mountain pastures to the shelter of the grassy valleys for the winter.

4
How Deer Feed

Deer sit for hours just chewing the cud. This is a wapiti or American elk.

Deer feed on plant material, grazing on grass and herbs, or browsing on shoots, twigs, leaves, flowers and fruits. Plant material is rather tough, and deer have a special way of dealing with it. They swallow it whole, storing it in a special part of the stomach called the **rumen**. This means that they can take in a lot of food in a short time, then retreat to the shelter of the bushes, where their enemies cannot see them.

The rumen contains millions of **bacteria** and other **microscopic** creatures far too small to see. They break down the tough plant fibers into substances that the deer can use. They also make the food softer for the deer to chew.

Later, the deer bring up balls of the stored food – called "cuds" – back into their mouths and chew it properly. Animals that do this are called ruminants. Deer may sit for hours just

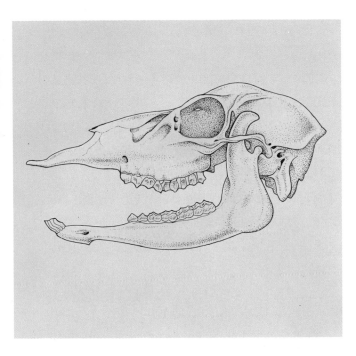

The skull of a deer showing the toothless space in the upper jaw.

A moose cow and her calf graze on lush grass near the edge of a lake.

chewing the cud.

Deer have no upper front teeth. Instead, there is a hard, gum-like pad. This toothless space allows the tongue to work around the food, mixing it with saliva, which contains juices that help to soften and break down the plant material. The large cheek teeth have a series of ridges, which crush the food. The tough plant material wears down the teeth, so they keep on growing throughout the deer's life.

5
Family Life

The huge bull moose lives alone for most of the year.

Living Together

Deer that live in dense forests usually live in small groups. They feed on particular trees and bushes that grow in small patches, so there would be squabbling if larger groups tried to feed in the same area. The huge bull moose, which may eat 9 kilograms (20 lb) of leaves a day, lives alone for much of the year.

Many woodland and forest deer keep to their own patch of forest, called their **territory**. Deer produce smelly fluids from special **glands** under the eyes, on the forehead, and sometimes even in the clefts in their hoofs. They rub this scent on the ground, and on twigs and branches, to mark the edges of their territory. The smell tells other deer that this patch of forest is already claimed.

Out in the open grassland there is little shelter, so the deer are more likely to be attacked by **predators**. Deer that feed here usually live in larger groups, where there is a better chance that one of the deer will spot a predator approaching and warn the rest of the herd.

Each deer knows its own place in the herd, and usually will not confront a bigger, stronger deer. This system prevents having too many fights within the group.

Deer use smell to recognize other members of their herd. They also use a wide range of sounds to communicate with each other. These range from whispers, grunts and moans, to bleating, clicking and even grinding their teeth.

A red deer stag with his harem of hinds. The males and females of many kinds of deer mix only during the rut.

The Rut

In the tropics, deer will mate and produce their young at any time of the year. But farther north and south, where the winters are cold, they usually mate in late summer or autumn and give birth to their young the following spring, when there is plenty of fresh young grass for them to feed on.

The males (called stags, bucks or **bulls**) and females (called **hinds** or **cows**) of many kinds of deer live in separate groups for most of the year. They come together to mate in the breeding season, called the **rut**. At this time, the females produce a special scent that attracts the males.

Two wapiti bulls fight for possession of a good rutting area.

A wapiti bull roars a challenge to rival males.

This fallow deer buck is rolling in mud on which he has squirted urine. This gives him a very strong smell and makes him attractive to females.

Stags in the rut become very restless, thrashing their antlers on trees and bushes, and pacing up and down without pausing to eat. Each stag selects an area of ground in which to collect a group of females – a **harem**. This is his rutting area.

Stags will fight over the best rutting areas. First, they challenge other stags by roaring at them. If one stag has a much louder roar than another stag, the weaker animal usually retreats without a fight. This prevents animals of unequal size from fighting and perhaps causing serious injuries. Stags with equally powerful roars may decide to fight. They charge at each other, heads down, until their antlers clash. Then, with their antlers, they push each other until one gives way. Often a fight takes so long that the hinds have wandered off by the time the winning stag returns to claim them!

Growing Up

Most deer produce one young one every year; moose and European elk usually have twins; and a few small deer produce up to six young at a time. Deer make poor fathers. After mating,

A white-tailed deer fawn stays very still as it waits for its mother to return. Its spotted coat helps to camouflage it.

the stags abandon the hinds until the next breeding season.

When the baby deer, called a **fawn**,

is born, it is still wet from being inside its mother. The mother licks it clean, so that it will not smell and attract predators.

Within a few minutes, the fawn is able to stand, and in a few hours it can walk. It feeds by sucking milk from its mother's **nipples**, between her back legs. The mother feeds it every few hours, then she leaves the fawn while she goes to find food for herself. The little fawn lies perfectly still, so an enemy will not notice it.

Older fawns play a lot with each other. Play helps to strengthen their tiny bodies and improve their movement skills.

By the end of the year, the fawn will have grown its adult coat, and will be feeding on grass and leaves by itself. It will stay close to its mother until she gives birth to the next fawn in the spring. Then she will drive it away. By now, female young will be ready to

An elk fawn feeds on its mother's milk. The milk is so rich that the fawn needs only a few drinks a day.

have young of their own, and the young males will be growing their first set of antlers.

6
Enemies and Friends

Wolves attack and kill deer in many parts of the world.

Predators and Helpmates

Deer suffer from illnesses just like other mammals do. Sometimes they catch diseases such as foot-and-mouth disease from farm animals. Mosquitoes bite deer just as they bite humans. Deer will often go and stand in water or in the sea, or move to windy hilltops to get away from mosquitoes and other biting flies.

They also suffer from **parasites** such as lice, which hide in their fur and bite or suck their blood. Botflies and warble flies lay their eggs in deer skin. Their maggots feed under the skin, often causing infected sores.

Hoofs are useful tools for scratching the skin to remove parasites. The tongue is also used to keep the fur clean. Some deer have such long tongues that they can clean their eyes with them. Deer also use their tongues and teeth to **groom**

each other's fur.

In the tropics, there are birds called oxpeckers, which land on the deer and feed on their skin parasites. Usually the deer put up with the oxpecker's attentions, and only shake their heads or stamp their feet to frighten them off if they get too close to eyes or ears.

Much more of a threat to many wild

A barasingha deer scratches itself with a hoof to get rid of parasites.

deer are other animals that hunt them as food. Wolves attack and kill deer in many parts of the world. Other large predators, such as bears, wild boar (pigs), tigers, mountain lions and, in some places, crocodiles, also kill and eat deer.

Camouflage and Defense

Although deer have many enemies, they survive mainly because they are difficult to see. Unless they feed in dense forest, they usually stay hidden among bushes and trees until the light is low in the evening and early morning. Then they come out to feed.

The color of their coats matches the color of their surroundings – they have good camouflage.

Most deer shed their coats twice a year. The thicker winter coat is often

This white-tailed buck is well camouflaged among the browns and grays of the autumn woodland.

paler and grayer than the summer coat. This provides a better camouflage against the snow and frost-covered ground, and blends with the winter woodlands and its bare tree trunks.

Many deer are a lighter color on their bellies than on their backs. Hunters recognize deer by their shape, which is often shown up by their shadows. In bright sunlight, the deer's bellies will be in shadow – darker than their backs. By having pale bellies, the effect of the shadow is lost. Baby deer are often spotted. The spots break up their outline and make them difficult to see. If frightened, fawns will "freeze," staying quite still, so their movements will not give them away.

Deer have other defenses, too. Male deer will defend themselves with their antlers, which often have sharp points. Deer will also use their hoofs to kick attackers.

Even in the distance the white rumps of these fallow deer are easily noticed. They serve as warning signals to be flashed to other members of the herd in times of danger.

Their excellent hearing and sense of smell gives them good warning of approaching danger. Deer can run very fast to escape danger.

Deer at Risk

Although deer have many natural enemies like wolves and bears, they usually allow some deer to survive. If deer become scarce, the predators

A Père David's deer in Woburn Abbey park, England. Some Père David's deer from China were taken to Britain early this century. When all the Chinese Père David's deer were killed, these were the only ones left in the world.

have nothing to eat, so their numbers decrease, too, and the deer numbers recover. But humans do not have this problem. Sometimes they kill too many deer, and that kind of deer disappears forever – it becomes **extinct**. Today nearly thirty kinds of deer are at risk of extinction.

Many deer have been saved by laws banning hunting. Where deer are killed for special purposes, such as using their velvet to make medicines, we are now learning how to farm them, so that wild deer are not killed. This has saved the musk deer of the Far East. It was killed for its musk, a scented fluid it produces in the breeding season, which is used in expensive perfumes and eastern medicines.

An even bigger threat comes from the loss of the deer's natural homes, as humans drain swamps and cut down forests and woodlands to make

farmland or to build cities. Now many countries are setting up deer reserves, where the natural vegetation is preserved, hunting is forbidden, and farm animals are kept out.

Some extremely rare deer have been saved from extinction because people took them to parks and zoos where they are now breeding successfully. The Père David's

A Key deer in the Florida Everglades. Once there were fewer than 300 Key deer because their swampy home was being drained for human settlement. Today they are protected by law and are safe from extinction.

deer has never been found in the wild. It has lived in royal parks in China for thousands of years.

7
Farming Deer

This trophy, a red deer stag's head, proves that the hunter is very skilled.

Deer and Humans

For thousands of years, humans have hunted deer. Pictures of deer have been found in cave paintings 14,000 years old. Their meat was eaten, the skins were used for clothing, and the antlers were used to make things, such as combs and axe handles.

Today, deer are still hunted for food in many parts of the world. They are also hunted for sport. The antlers are hung on walls. Owning a fine set of antlers shows that the hunter has the skill to shoot a large stag. In some parts of the world, hunting has encouraged people to keep deer in special parks and to protect them by laws to make sure there are still plenty left to hunt. Deer parks have existed since Roman times in Europe, and even longer in China.

In the Far East, antlers are used in medicines. The velvet that surrounds the growing antlers is sold as an **aphrodisiac**.

In many countries, deer are farmed like cattle. They have even been introduced to Australia and New Zealand for farming. Deer can do well on poor land where the grass is not

These European elk are being farmed in China for their velvet.

Deer are so common in some parts of the world that they will even come into gardens in search of food.

good enough for cattle. Most are bred for their meat, which is very tasty and lean, and sometimes for their antlers and velvet, too.

Deer are also kept simply because they are beautiful to look at. Many rare deer have been brought to parks to interest visitors. Sometimes, this has saved them from extinction.

Reindeer and Caribou

Arctic people like the Inuit (Eskimos) and Canadian Indians have hunted caribou and reindeer for thousands of years. The meat is dried or frozen for use during the winter, the females may be milked, the skins used for clothing, the antlers for tools, and the animals themselves can be used to carry heavy loads and pull sleds.

The Yakuts of Siberia and the Lapps from the U.S.S.R and Scandinavia move with the herds. In winter the reindeer feed in the forests or on the lower mountain slopes. In spring they travel about 320 kilometers (199 mi) to the coast, or to higher mountain pastures. During this spring migration, the reindeer cows give birth to their calves. This is a dangerous time, and the Lapps have to keep a look out for foxes and eagles, which might kill the newborn calves.

A Norwegian Lapp sells reindeer skins at the roadside. Once the Lapps dressed in reindeer skin tunics and leggings, but today they prefer brightly colored clothes.

By late August, the herds start to move to their winter pastures. In mid-September, the bulls round up harems of cows ready for the rut, and pushing contests between bulls are common. In October, the reindeer mate.

Once the rut is over, the Lapps round up their reindeer, driving them into pens. Here, they sort out stray

Lapps travel with their reindeer on their spring and autumn migrations.

animals from other herds, clip the ears of the new calves to identify them, and decide which animals will be killed. These will generally be bulls that are too old to breed, or weak animals unlikely to survive the winter. They provide meat for the Lapp family and skins to sell.

8
Learning More About Deer

Red deer droppings in the forest. Deer droppings are short and oval or round, often with a point at one end.

Deer are very difficult to see in the wild. They are extremely shy, and usually remain hidden except at dawn and dusk, when the light is dim. Even when they venture out to feed, their coats blend with the background, making them difficult to detect. Their excellent hearing and good sense of smell means that they will usually know you are there long before you see them, and they are surprisingly good at just disappearing.

However, it is not difficult to find signs that deer are around. In the snow, and on muddy paths and in soft ground around the edges of ponds and ditches, you may find their footprints. A guide book of animal tracks will explain how to tell the kind of deer, the direction it was traveling, and whether it was walking or running. You may also find tufts of hairs caught on a thorn bush or wire fence. Look on the ground for deer droppings, and for flattened grass where a deer has lain hidden.

Stags and bucks rub their antlers against trees and bushes to remove the velvet, and later in the rut they will thrash their antlers in the undergrowth, leaving broken twigs and fraying bark.

Try visiting one of the many parks and zoos that keep deer. This will help you to recognize the deer if you later find them in the wild. You may also be lucky enough to see deer from other countries.

A track of a white-tailed deer in North Carolina. Deer tracks are like pairs of crescent-shaped dents.

This tree trunk has been shredded by deer. They fray the bark with their antlers. Deer also eat bark.

Two red deer hinds in the early morning mist. Deer are difficult to see in the wild because they are naturally shy, preferring to come out to feed at dawn or dusk.

Glossary

Adapted Changed so as to become better suited to a particular way of life.

Antlers Branching, bony outgrowths from the skull that are produced once a year during the breeding season, then shed. Usually only the males have antlers.

Aphrodisiac A substance that causes people to fall in love with each other.

Bacteria Minute living creatures too small to see.

Breeding season A particular time of year when animals mate to produce young.

Browsers Animals that feed on bushes and trees.

Buck A male deer.

Bull The name given to the males of very large deer such as caribou, reindeer, moose and European elk.

Camouflage A color or pattern that matches the background and makes the animal difficult to see.

Court To behave in such a way as to attract a mate.

Cow The name given to the females of very large deer such as caribou, reindeer, moose and European elk.

Extinct Having died out completely.

Fawn A baby deer.

Glands A part of the body that produces special substances that are used somewhere else in the body or outside it.

Grazing Feeding on grass and other plants growing on the ground.

Groom To lick, scratch and smooth the fur to clean it.

Harem A group of females belonging to a particular male.

Hind A female deer.

Lichens Small crusty or leafy growths that cling to tree trunks or form carpets on bare ground.

Mammals Warm-blooded animals with hair or fur, the females of which produce milk to feed their young.

Microscopic Something so small that it can only be seen with a microscope.

Migrate The act of traveling regularly from one place to another at a certain time of year.

Molting Shedding the fur or hair from time to time. Hairs are lost one at a time, and new hairs grow, so the animal is never hairless.

Nipples Small teats on the bellies of female mammals through which the young suck milk.

Parasites Creatures that live and feed on other living creatures.

Predators Animals that kill and eat other animals.

Rumen The first part of the stomach of ruminants in which food is partly digested.

Rut The part of the deer's breeding season when the males fight over and mate with the females.

Sedges Grass-like plants with stiff leaves that grow in threes around the stem.

Stag A male deer.

Territory A piece of land occupied by a particular animal that defends it and tries to stop other animals from coming into it.

Tundra A vast area of flat treeless land where the soil is always frozen.

Velvet The thin layer of skin and soft velvety fur that covers the antlers while they are growing.

Finding Out More

The following books will tell you more about deer.

The Caribou by Jerolyn Nentl. Crestwood House, 1984.

The Little Deer of the Florida Keys by Hope Ryden. Florida Classics, 1985.

Mammals by Tessa Board. Franklin Watts, 1983.

Mammals and How They Live by Robert M. McClung. Random House, 1963.

Mother Deer and Her Spotted Fawns by Juana Chavez. Pueblo Acoma Press, 1981.

Mule Deer by Colleen Bare. Dodd, 1981.

The Whitetail by Mark Ahlstrom. Crestwood House, 1983.

The World of the White-Tailed Deer by Leonard L. Rue. Harper and Row, 1962.

Index

Picture acknowledgments

The photographs in this book were supplied by:
B. & C. Alexander 39; Bruce Coleman Ltd: Gerald Cubitt 8; Oxford Scientific Films: Jill Bailey 17 (bottom), 38, 41 (left); Maria M. Boyd 31, 34; David Cayless 36, 42; M.J. Coe 41 (right); J.A.L. Cooke 21; Harry Engels 16; Sally Foy 19 (top); David C. Fritts (Animals Animals) 14, 18, 20; Steven Fuller (Animals Animals) 22; Terry Heathcoate 25, 37, (left), 40; Zig Leszczynski 19 (bottom), 35; Stephen Mills 33; Stan Osolinski *cover* 23, 24, 26, 27 (left), 29; Charles Palek 15 (right); Partridge Productions Ltd. 17 (top); C.M. Perrins 37 (right); Press-tige Pictures 13 (right); Ray Richardson (Animals Animals) 9; Leonard Lee Rue III (Animals Animals) 10, 12, 13 (left), 28, 32; Alastair Shay, *frontispiece*, 11, 27 (right); Stouffer Productions Ltd. 30; M. Wilding 15 (left). The illustrations on pages 9, 11 and 23 are by John Yates.